Jarrold Colour Publications, Norwich

Introduction

The Cotswold Hills extend from Bath in Avon to Chipping Campden in Gloucestershire, rising to 600 feet in places, and never exceeding thirty miles in breadth. Surrounding them is one of the finest areas of unspoilt countryside in England – an area with delightfully preserved villages and historic houses, splendid gardens and castles, great abbeys and cathedrals, and well-stocked wildlife parks.

Yet all these varied attractions are linked by a common factor which gives them a distinctive 'Cotswold' appearance – they have largely been constructed with the local honey-coloured stone. The result is a warm, rich landscape, intersected by straight Roman roads which invite the visitor to explore further.

The area known as the Cotswolds actually derives its name from the Anglo-Saxon words 'cote', meaning sheepfold, and 'wold', meaning a piece of open, uncultivated land, downs or woods. Sheep have indeed played an important part in the region's history since as far back as the thirteenth century when Cistercian monks began to rear them there. Much of the wealth that is in evidence in the area today has been created by the woollen industry, and the abundance of magnificent churches and gracious manor houses serves to emphasize the affluence created in the area by sheep-farming; although its importance has declined a little over the years.

Previous Page: *Chipping Campden*. Below: *Berkeley Castle*

Above: *Sunset over the Rushy Pen, Slimbridge*
Right: *Mandarin Drake*
(Photographs by kind permission of Lady Scott)

The Western Edge

In the far south-west of the region is Berkeley Castle. This perfectly preserved stronghold overlooking the River Severn has been the home of the Berkeleys since it was begun in 1153 and is still lived in by the family today. The massive Norman keep, dungeon, great hall and kitchen all date from the twelfth century but alterations were made in 1340. However, the room in the dungeons where Edward II was brutally murdered in 1327 remains exactly as it was at the time of his death. Less macabre attractions including paintings, tapestries, fine furniture and silver.

A few miles further north and providing a stark contrast to Berkeley is the Wildfowl Trust just one mile to the north-west of Slimbridge, Gloucestershire. The largest and most varied collection of waterfowl in the world can be seen in this low-lying area, just west of the Cotswold Hills, which reaches out in flats and marshes towards the wide meanders of the River Severn as it flows into its tidal estuary. The Trust was founded by Sir Peter Scott in 1946 and few sights today can rival the spectacular arrival of thousands of wild geese finding sanctuary in the Severn Estuary.

Heading further north-east is the delightful town of Painswick with its close-built houses lining steep streets. Painswick is an old wool town dating back to the fourteenth century and in its parish churchyard there are more than 100 clipped yews, some of which have been there since 1714. Traditionally, there were only ninety-nine trees, and it is said that every time the hundredth was planted, the Devil removed it.

Another Cotswold cloth town is Minchinhampton, situated high up on the eastern edge of Minchinhampton Common, a 580 acre area managed by the National Trust. It has a number of interesting buildings, including a fascinating market house supported on rows of stone and wood columns, and a church with a fine fourteenth-century south transept and an unusually truncated spire which was taken down to its current height in 1563.

Left: *Painswick*
Below: *Minchinhampton*

Two of the principal towns of the western edge are Cheltenham and Stroud. Cheltenham is one of the foremost spa towns in England, having the country's only alkaline spring rising in the Cheltenham Ladies College. The waters can still be sampled at the Town Hall, Pump Room and at a number of hotels. The Duke of Wellington is said to have found the waters beneficial to a liver complaint and recommended that his officers sampled them.

The superb sweeping crescents and elaborate ironwork balconies of Regency houses dominate Cheltenham, and the Pittville Pump Room, with its colonnade and dome, is arguably the town's most beautiful building. Splendid floral gardens complement the graceful atmosphere of this delightful spa town.

Stroud, with its quaint steep streets, nestles at the junction of five valleys. It became a wool town after Flemish weavers settled there in Elizabethan times and laid the foundations for a flourishing cloth industry. High quality cloth is still produced, including billiard table cloth, and the town itself has retained considerable character despite industrialisation in the late eighteenth and early nineteenth centuries. The Town Hall, for example, has a sixteenth-century Tudor façade.

Left: *Cheltenham.* Below: *Stroud*

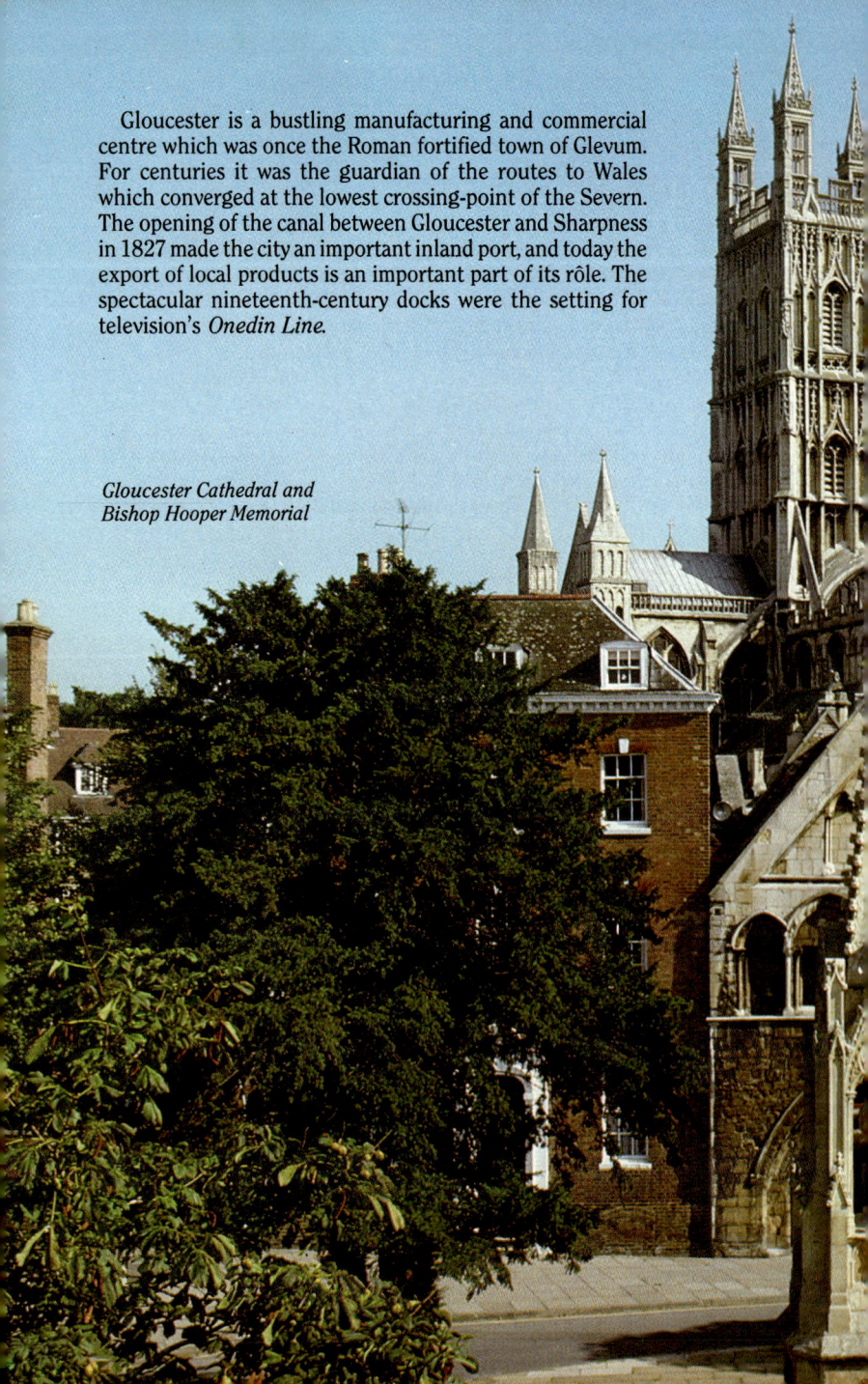

Gloucester is a bustling manufacturing and commercial centre which was once the Roman fortified town of Glevum. For centuries it was the guardian of the routes to Wales which converged at the lowest crossing-point of the Severn. The opening of the canal between Gloucester and Sharpness in 1827 made the city an important inland port, and today the export of local products is an important part of its rôle. The spectacular nineteenth-century docks were the setting for television's *Onedin Line*.

Gloucester Cathedral and Bishop Hooper Memorial

This old, historic city is dominated by the tall, square tower of the majestic Perpendicular cathedral. Gloucester Abbey was founded in AD 681 but it was not until 1331 that the construction of the cathedral began. Fourteen years later work began on the fan vaulting of the cloisters with their superbly delicate tracery. The cathedral's east window measures 72 feet by 38 feet, making it the second largest medieval stained glass window in the country, after York Minster. It was made in about 1350 to commemorate Edward III's victory at the Battle of Crecy in 1344.

Gloucester has many other fascinating buildings and a walkway called the Via Sacra links the more interesting sites. The half-timbered Bishop Hooper's Lodging houses an interesting Folk Museum and is well worth a visit.

North Cotswold Classics

The northern area of the Cotswolds contains some of its best-known and most-loved villages. Winchcombe, for example, nestles in the wooded valley of the River Isbourne, just below the Cotswold Scarp. It is hard to believe that this peaceful little town was once the capital of the ancient Kingdom of Mercia. A great abbey founded here in AD 797 caused Winchcombe to become a place of pilgrimage in medieval times, but the abbey was quickly destroyed after the Dissolution. The George Inn, which was once a pilgrim's hostel, is now one of the few remaining reminders of the abbey. The parish church with its forty grotesque gargoyles houses an altar cloth embroidered by Henry VIII's first wife, Catherine of Aragon.

Nearby Sudeley Castle also has connections with one of Henry VIII's many wives – this time, Catherine Parr, his sixth Queen. She is buried at the castle because, in 1547, after Henry's death, she married her former lover, Lord Seymour of Sudeley. Unfortunately, she died during childbirth just a year after her marriage, and the castle's chapel became her final resting-place.

The castle has had a varied history: it was the headquarters for Charles I during the Civil War and was besieged in 1643 and again in 1644. In complete contrast, it now houses the largest private collection of toys and dolls on general view in the whole of Europe.

Left: *Vineyard Street, Winchcombe*. Below: *Sudeley Castle*

Stanton and Stanway are beautifully unspoilt villages situated below the wooded Cotswold edge. Stanton, the furthest north of the two, was lovingly restored by Sir Phillip Stott in the early 1900s, and his own house, Stanton Court, is a fine example of a beautifully-kept Jacobean home.

The Church of St Michael and All Angels has a well-proportioned Perpendicular tower and spire but its Norman origins are revealed inside by the north arcade. Sir Ninian Comper restored this medieval place of worship and some of his own stained glass has been incorporated into the structure.

A mile further south is the small village of Stanway lying at the foot of Stanway Hill. Stanton and Stanway seem almost to compete with each other for fine buildings and their respective churches have numerous points of interest. The church in Stanway, for example, has a Jacobean pulpit and a beautiful bronze by Alexander Fisher, and the fine Jacobean manor house stands in lovely gardens beneath steep, wooded parklands.

Nearby Snowshill with its charming Tudor manor is also well worth a visit. The manor's genteel William and Mary facade hides a veritable Aladdin's cave of treasures including clocks, musical instruments, armour (including Samurai armour), scientific instruments, spinning wheels and fire-fighting equipment!

Below: *Stanton.* Right: *Snowshill Manor*

At the far north of the Cotswolds is one of Britain's most famous villages – the show village of Broadway. Its long central street with broad greens and magnificent Elizabethan houses has long been a major attraction of the area, and indeed, many of the fine houses have now been adapted to the needs of tourists: there is an abundance of hotels, tea-shops and antique shops. These, of course, bear close inspection and a leisurely stroll along the broad main street is a delightful way to spend an afternoon. But the charm of Broadway can also be appreciated from the high ground above the village at Broadway Beacon. Broadway Tower, a folly built in 1800, sits at 1,024 feet above sea level. On a fine day fourteen counties can be seen from its castellated roof, with the Black Mountains in the far west and the Berkshire Downs in the south.

Moreton-in-Marsh lies to the southeast of Broadway and is a busy old market town lying astride the broad Fosse Way which was built by the Romans. Like Broadway, the town is built almost entirely along an exceptionally wide, grass-verged main street. The name of the town may refer to its position near the 'march' or boundary of Gloucestershire; some two miles distant is a stone column which marks the meeting-place of three counties.

In the heart of Moreton-in-Marsh stands a little sixteenth-century Curfew Tower which is well worth a visit, as is an elegant eighteenth-century house to the east of the church. Take time to look around these towns – you will not be disappointed!

Right: *Typical Cotswold architecture in Broadway*
Inset: *Broadway Tower*

Chipping Campden is a delightfully unspoilt town, with buildings dating from every century since the fourteenth. The many and varied styles blend harmoniously, however, because they are practically all built of honey-coloured Cotswold stone. In the fourteenth and fifteenth centuries Chipping Campden was one of the most prosperous and important centres of the wool trade and the buildings which can be seen today reflect that affluence.

There are fourteenth-century houses and inns, a fifteenth-century grammar school, seventeenth-century almshouses and Market Hall, and an eighteenth-century Town Hall. The lovely Market Hall, now in the care of the National Trust, was once the meeting-place for the buying and selling of wool, and the word 'chipping' is derived from the old word 'ceapen' or 'market'.

At the other end of the High Street to the Market Hall are the seventeenth-century almshouses built by Sir Baptist Hicks, one of the great benefactors of Chipping Campden. These almshouses were restored by Guy Pemberton in 1953. Close to them is the magnificent Perpendicular Church of St James, whose tower is one of the finest in the country. Traces of Norman and thirteenth-century stonework are visible in the church but the tower itself dates from the fifteenth century.

Sir Baptist Hicks also built Campden House, just to the south of the church, but in 1645 he ordered it to be burned down rather than have it fall into the hands of the Parliamentarians. The gateway is one of the few parts to have survived.

Chipping Campden

The Heart of the Cotswolds

An air of Cotswolds gentility pervades Chipping Norton, the highest town in the county of Oxfordshire, more than 700 feet above sea level. It was mentioned in Domesday Book as Norton; the 'chipping' or 'ceapen' meaning market (as at Chipping Campden) was added to the name in the thirteenth century.

The town is built on west-facing slopes with a large Victorian tweed mill conspicuous in the valley, but it is dominated by a handsome nineteenth-century Town Hall. Near St Mary's Church, which has an unusual polygonal porch, there is a row of quaint almshouses which were built in 1640.

Stow-on-the-Wold is also situated more than 700 feet above sea level, hence the name by which it is affectionately known: 'Stow-on-the-Wold where the winds blow cold'.

The large Market Place is quaintly irregular, lined with pleasant old houses, inns and shops in a delightful variety of styles, and there is also an old Market Cross. The church contains a huge painting of the Crucifixion by de Craeyer. The town, like so many others in the Cotswolds, owes much of its prosperity to the woollen trade. Indeed, Daniel Defoe records that the year he came to Stow Fair, 20,000 sheep were sold.

Above: *Chipping Norton*. Right: *Stow-on-the-Wold*

Blenheim Palace, just south of Woodstock in Oxfordshire is a magnificent palace set in a fantastic 2500-acre park. It was the nation's gift to the 1st Duke of Marlborough and it was built between 1705–22. Sir John Vanbrugh designed the mansion in Baroque style, arranging the two storeys around three sides of an immense courtyard. The large central building has four turrets and a portico supported by Corinthian columns, and the overall effect is one of breathtaking grandeur.

Henry Wise, gardener to Queen Anne, designed the beautifully formal gardens in the early eighteenth century. The park contains an impressive bridge which sweeps across a huge lake with sweeping banks, allowing visitors to obtain an excellent view of the palace itself.

The state apartments house fine collections of portraits, china, tapestries and furniture. Tucked amongst all this grandeur on the ground floor is the small bedroom where Sir Winston Churchill was born on 30 November 1874. He was buried in this area too, in the quiet churchyard at Bladon, one mile south of Woodstock.

Woodstock itself is well worth a visit, having as it does a wonderful assortment of seventeenth- and eighteenth-century houses. The Town Hall there was built in 1766 and is worth a special mention.

Blenheim Palace

Rhino at the Cotswold Wild Life Park, near Burford

Such is the versatility of the Cotswolds that even tigers and leopards can look at home there! At the Cotswold Wild Life Park, near Burford, rhinos, zebras and ostriches roam in large paddocks bounded by unobtrusive moats. The tigers and leopards play happily in spacious, grassed enclosures, and in an old walled garden, tropical birds such as flamingoes and toucans enjoy life right in the heart of the Cotswolds.

This large and varied collection of animals and birds blends harmoniously with the peaceful and natural surroundings of the Cotswold Hills. It is set in 120 acres of gardens and parkland around a Gothic style manor house which was first opened in 1969. In addition to the outdoor attractions there is a tropical house which exhibits alligators, birds and a fascinating array of tropical plants. There is also a reptile house, aquarium, butterfly house, adventure playground, narrow gauge railway, brass-rubbing centre and pony rides. The Cotswold Wild Life Park is open daily throughout the year except Christmas Day.

Nearby Burford has an impressively wide main street dropping down into the Windrush valley. The river itself is crossed by a fine medieval bridge, and the town also has an interesting church with a Norman tower capped by a slender fifteenth-century spire.

The River Windrush winds its way through the delightful village of Bourton-on-the-Water (pictured overleaf). The river flows down the main street under low footbridges beside various trees and lawns, and has led to the village earning itself the somewhat inappropriate title of the 'Venice of the Cotswolds'. There is a model village built of Cotswold stone as a perfect reproduction of Bourton itself. It is built to one-tenth scale and it took six men four years to construct.

Bourton-on-the-Water's many attractions include a perfumery, Birdland, a motor museum and a model railway.

Just outside Bourton-on-the-Water are the delightful twin villages of Upper and Lower Slaughter. Both contain several buildings of interest and give an overall impression of English countryside at its best.

Upper Slaughter has a late Norman church which was restored in 1877, and nearby are eight cottages, grouped around a square, which were re-modelled by Lutyens in 1906. Although the manor house at Upper Slaughter has a two-storied Jacobean porch, it is otherwise a superb example of Elizabethan architecture. It is difficult to believe that this now peaceful village was the scene of much serious fighting in 1643 during the Great Rebellion.

Although a small tributary of the Windrush runs through Upper Slaughter it is Lower Slaughter which seems to have been built upon its banks, with the two sides being linked by a series of small bridges. The water used to drive the Old Mill but nowadays it is decorative rather than functional.

The thirteenth-century church of St Mary was almost entirely rebuilt in 1867 but it retains its original nave arcade and it also has a most beautiful modern reredos depicting the Crucifixion. Beside the church stands the manor, with an intriguing dovecot built like a many-gabled house.

Left: *Upper Slaughter.* Below: *Lower Slaughter*

Naunton is yet another long, thin village of typical Cotswold stone houses spread out along the floor of the deep Windrush valley. The church has a handsome Perpendicular tower with pinnacles, gargoyles, a white stone pulpit and an old Saxon cross. It was considerably restored in 1878.

Of Naunton's old manor house there remains only a fifteenth-century four-gabled dovecot with almost 2,000 nesting boxes. Ironically, the dove is a bird of peace, and although this seems entirely appropriate for the serene village of Naunton as seen today, the Cotswolds have not always been so peaceful. Indeed, the monument to William Oldys in the church 'who for his loyalty to his king and zeal for ye Established Church was barbarously murther'd by ye Rebells in ye year 1645', reminds us of bloodier times.

A little further west at Guiting Power, more animals can be found, this time of a more domestic nature, at the Cotswold Farm Park. In a beautiful farm setting high on top of the Cotswolds, a wide selection of rare farm breeds are on show, including Longhorn cattle and Soay and Orkney sheep.

Below: *Naunton.* Right: *Gloucester Old Spot pigs at the Cotswold Farm Park, Guiting Power*

Heading South

In the far south-east of the Cotswolds is the pretty town of Lechlade with its streets of Georgian houses. It takes its name from the River Leach which joins the Thames beside the Trout Inn just below St John's Bridge. Lechlade Bridge is known as Halfpenny Bridge from the days when there was a halfpenny toll, and today this is the highest navigable point on the Thames for cabin cruisers. A huge part of the surrounding area forms the Cotswold Water Park, where old gravel workings form linked lakes and ponds now being developed for water recreation of every description.

Further north, just off the A361, is the Oxfordshire village of Westwell which is set in a little wooded hollow teeming with picturesque cottages, heavily laden with old-fashioned climbing plants. The church, rectory and manor house look out across a rough green, complete with pond, and the resulting scene is serenely idyllic.

The church, which has a quaint wooden turret, dates from Norman times and stands amongst fascinating tombs. Inside the church there is an attractive seventeenth-century monument to the Trinder family.

Below: *Lechlade*. Right: *Westwell*

The River Leach separates another set of twin villages – those of Eastleach Martin and Eastleach Turville, both of which are set in beautifully rural positions. Each has a parish church separated by only 250 yards and linked across the water by a stone footbridge known as 'Keble's Bridge' after the poet John Keble who was minister of both churches for eight years in the nineteenth century. The banks of the Leach are scattered with daffodils in the spring, making this whole area seem even more enchanting.

Almost due west and nestled in another river valley, that of the River Coln, is the village of Bibury, which is famous for its row of fifteenth-century lichen-covered cottages, known as Arlington Row.

Nearby is the heavily buttressed seventeenth-century Arlington Mill, which has now been transformed into a working museum where the machinery still turns to delight visitors.

Below: *Keble's Bridge between Eastleach Martin and Eastleach Turville*
Right: *Arlington Row, Bibury*

Cirencester

To complete this brief tour of the Cotswolds, it is worth taking a look at one of its largest and most important towns – Cirencester. This old town, which was called Corinium by the Romans, was, after London, the largest town in Britain in the second century. Three Roman roads, Akeman Street, the Fosse Way and Ermine Street, still radiate from Cirencester today, and excavations have revealed many exciting Roman finds. The Corinium Museum houses many of these finds and a few miles to the north is the extensive Chedworth Roman Villa.

Cirencester, like so many other Cotswold towns and villages featured here, is a pleasing blend of old and new. Old-fashioned charm coupled with modern facilities make this heart of England a most attractive area to visit.

Text by Jane Bulmer.